DOG AND MOON

ᐅᒐᐸ

OSKANA POETRY & POETICS

Kelly Shepherd

Dog and Moon

 University of Regina Press

Printed and bound in Canada at Imprimerie Gauvin. The text of this book is printed on 100% post-consumer recycled paper with earth-friendly vegetable-based inks.

Cover art: "Moon is reflected in a wavy water" by korionov / Adobe Stock

Cover and text design: Duncan Campbell, University of Regina Press

Series Editor: Randy Lundy
Copy Editor: Kelly Laycock

The text and titling faces are Arno, designed by Robert Slimbach.

Library and Archives Canada Cataloguing in Publication

Title: Dog and moon / Kelly Shepherd.

Names: Shepherd, Kelly, 1974- author

Series: Oskana poetry & poetics.

Description: Series statement: Oskana poetry & poetics | Poems.

Identifiers: Canadiana (print) 20240457269 | Canadiana (ebook) 20240457277 | ISBN 9781779400383 (softcover) | ISBN 9781779400413 (EPUB) | ISBN 9781779400406 (PDF)

Subjects: LCGFT: Poetry.

Classification: LCC PS8637.H4765 D64 2025 | DDC C811/.6—dc23

10 9 8 7 6 5 4 3 2 1

UNIVERSITY OF REGINA PRESS
University of Regina
Regina, Saskatchewan
Canada S4S 0A2
TELEPHONE: (306) 585-4758
FAX: (306) 585-4699
WEB: www.uofrpress.ca
EMAIL: uofrpress@uregina.ca

We acknowledge the support of the Canada Council for the Arts for our publishing program. We acknowledge the financial support of the Government of Canada. / Nous reconnaissons l'appui financier du gouvernement du Canada. This publication was made possible with support from Creative Saskatchewan's Book Publishing Production Grant Program.

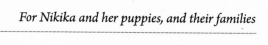

For Nikika and her puppies, and their families

CONTENTS

II. The Hidden Mystery School Is Holding an Open House

III. To Become Worthy of the Ocean

I

THE RAVEN-NECKLACED SKY

A man walks out of the forest. What walks out of him?
A good question is a snail, carrying its own answer on its back.

Making a home inside. Words are little houses;
words are caves. The man walks into the city,

but before he gets there, the city has already walked into him.
When he was young, people thought he had feathers

on his head instead of hair. Fable is a verb: from *fabulari*, to talk.
Many years later, it turned out to be leaves:

the new green you see after fire or rain. Green fire.
What is magic but the process of making something

that has become dull incandesce again?
A lie breathed through silver. Descending into the unconscious

and following those who know more than we do. Feathers, leaves—
now that the man is a baby again, no one is certain.

Fish grow leafy fins and tails. Trees grow fish-shaped leaves.
The trees, water, fire of childhood.

Water becomes wind; wind becomes water.
Everything in nature swims; everything in nature flies.

Nothing in nature has more symbolic value
than the roots of trees. With the possible exception of fish.

Spawning salmon turn creek water red and gold and brown,
the colour of rusty apples. The metamemories of childhood.

No camera can capture it precisely because it is a verb.
The root is the mysterious tree, says Gaston Bachelard.

It is the subterranean, inverted tree. For the root,
the darkest earth is also a mirror, and fish swim inside mirrors.

SELFIE

Mirrors and magpies
recognize and respect one another.

When poets stopped using paper,
symbols made them nervous.

Mirrors became nothing more
than places to point cameras.

Magpies are not so easily domesticated.
A dog is an ancient mythical symbol

a man puts on a leash.
Anyone can be a writer.

So what is freewriting? Dog and moon wake each other up.
If water is the mind, it is turbid with rememberings.

Patterns that don't closely enough resemble patterns.
The idea is that you write without thinking too hard about it.

The lake is the same green as the floating willow leaves:
brightness born of night-coloured walls.

Describe the physical experience of submerging in water.
Pollen ignites in the sun all around me, all the way down to the sand.

I swim in pure green. Music in the skin that won't settle on a melody.
A dark pool of feeling that something has been forgotten.

The numbness behind the eyes, before or after a headache.
That movement in the corner, the damp shadow, was a toad.

What had it come up from the earth to say?
The mind struggles with the mind—Mars is at its brightest.

THERE ARE MOUNTAINS
HIDDEN IN MOUNTAINS

Sunset: a sickle rusted with clouds.
The kind of moon that cuts the sky.

Did we pray to the gods who would eat us
by eating them?

One day a year, the river changes direction.
On some rivers, the year does:

salmon and fishermen watch one another closely.
We are not returning

to the oldest human beliefs.
We never left.

A fork has four beginnings and one end,
or one beginning, and four ends.

Knives and spoons are less complicated,
but they tell better stories.

To poison a nation, says Ben Okri, you poison its stories.
Another option is to poison the water.

Sigmund Freud first went to school to become a petroleum engineer.
Have you ever actually looked at their drawings?

Listen: if a loud noise can bring something to life, it was never dead.
But the sound quality has to be just right.

Ask the jazz singer in the stairwell. Ask the stairwell.
A northern flicker drums on a metal lamppost,

and all the other street lights turn their heads to look.
The musician practised for hours every day.

After six months, the viola started to grow feathers.
After three years, it was a Canada goose. It flew away.

By the time the bus arrives, the raven
across the street has become three ravens.

They are still searching for the third thing.
Time is like a river, now speeding up, now slowing down.

Again, just follow the breath. As you do, thoughts will arise.
Don't be bothered by them. A journey of a thousand miles

begins with a single schlep. That building was once a tower—
but the weight of the prairie sky.

When you take a step, the house moves
under the balls of your feet. It rolls with no sound

from one square side to another.
A wall becomes the floor, the ceiling becomes a wall.

There's a scratching. Some uncertainty.
That's the feeling of the dark on your skin.

A PISTACHIO NUT, THE SEED OF
A FRUIT WE DO NOT EAT, IS A LITTLE,
DRY, SALTLESS OYSTER

Its shell is smooth; its skin is a map.
I remember when this was a farmer's field;

now the tree-to-building height ratio is all wrong.
The poem is a house: open the door,

and walk down the hall. Gaston Bachelard told us
where to look: in cabinets and seashells.

Just before you go to sleep, the air in your room
turns grey as a dove. The stairwells fill up with pepper.

I prefer the onomatopoeic style of interior design.
Our blinds were open: we saw the flash

from the kitchen table. There was no rain, no storm.
Of the whole circle of matching beige-

vinyl-siding duplexes, the sky chose that place.
I want to make myself an empty room.

A house is a machine for living in, said Le Corbusier.
"Smart Homes Are No Longer a Gimmick—

They're the Only Way Forward."
Walking is an indicator species

for various kinds of freedoms and pleasures,
says Rebecca Solnit: free time,

free and alluring space, and unhindered bodies.
O plants, how I envy you your sensuous chlorophyll!

One ten-minute joyride to space
produces as much carbon dioxide in ten minutes

as thirty average humans emit in a year.
No poppy for me, thank you.

Art survives within modern civilization
rather like little islands of wilderness

saved to show us where we come from.
Pay attention to the enjambment of clouds in the wind.

SURFACE TENSION

There is green in the watery clouds.
The frog gods speak.

There is something heavy,
waterlogged with drowsiness

between and behind my eyes.
The round pool closes

and opens again when I blink.
The cattails on this side

brush up against the willows on that.
In this version of the story,

the princess throws him against the wall
instead of kissing him.

How's this for a rainy-day haiku:
The pond just got tired of waiting.

Dragonfly nymphs climb out of the water,
emerge as adults. Leave exoskeletons behind.

Evaporation, exuviae. Metamorphosis,
inevitability, passage through time and space.

Resisting closure. Breath of silt and mud.
Relationships of static bodies with dynamic bodies.

The river symbolizes only itself.
Why do I feel like this memory

has been right below the surface all this time?
Afric McGlinchey: A poem can be in two places at once.

A poem is a torch with a beam of shadow
instead of light. And memories for batteries.

A stone axe buried in a prairie field.
Heavy clouds, a feather of time before sunrise.

To be lunar means to change, says Sophie Strand.
A bear carved out of amber. The long labour of art.

A rodent's nest in a chest of drawers.
A little myth. Evening is a pot of stew.

Keep it simple. This is not a hero's journey.
Add more wood. Morning is the fire.

As for the storytellers, the birds of sorrow.
They migrate at night and navigate using the stars.

Measuring the circadian rhythms of poplar trees:
silver-green trunks and leaf music in the breeze.

Smooth to the touch. A thousand thousand butterflies
dancing the Maypole. A green school of anchovies

flashing in sunlight, spiralling upward into the shape of a tree.
A tent. With crooked walls, sleep

is a narrow hallway that just keeps getting narrower and narrower.
I wasn't sure if I heard loons, or coyotes—

her breathing in the morning. The hills have nettle-coloured eyes.
Everything is overgrown, and overgreen.

The smell of hot air under spruce trees.
Gathering dry dead branches—scraped knuckles.

Scaly bark and the soft skin of wrists.
The fire with its breaking-twig voice.

Your clothes smell like campfire. Stars are still visible
over treetops. Throughout the night they turn, then fade.

You turn when you hear movement:
you stand face to face with two spotted fawns.

Their faces are close to yours: your entire night
inside the tent is in their eyes.

Newborn sun, cottonwood bark, yellowed reeds, dark
river mud in their fur. You know it would be soft to touch.

Don't be afraid of us, we're always saying to other animals.
A constellation in its infancy:

the fawns turn and fade out of sight.
Your coffee cools. You stand on river-smoothed stones.

Smooth stones hurt my bare feet, it's that early in the season.
Fingerlings swim between water striders

and their six-circled shadows. Cattails, shallow water,
spongy mud deeper than a paddle will push.

Marshy shore, horsetail ferns, ancient eyes of dragonflies.
The sunrise stops and waits in willow leaves.

Current-crumpled green and brown—wet leaves among rocks—
baby frogs. Nature isn't nature: it's language.

A bend in the stream, and in the musical notes of rushing water.
Uncommon and local in marshes, where it hides among reeds

and grasses. Its cryptic plumage blends in with the vegetation.
What's that army helicopter doing in my nature poem?

Memory: its morning-coloured leaves are lush,
and its night-coloured wings are many

so that you can't ever see through it, you can't see further
back in time, no matter how long you look.

Spirits of storms bring the morning,
and morning rain falls from their black wings.

Crows know only the shadows of songs.
But aren't shadows symbols of the soul?

What a strange machine man is, wrote Nikos Kazantzakis.
You fill him with bread, wine, fish, and radishes,

and out comes sighs, laughter, and dreams.
Morning: a cool forest rain whispers in mist

beneath the thousand-petalled sun. You understand
this language with your skin, not your ears. It is untranslatable.

The words move like insects, black ants, around the page.
Another cup of meltwater, please!

It snowed for forty days and forty nights.
The city is completely quiet. Only dogs are happy.

But there is a new city beneath the city:
human-sized tunnels have been excavated under the snow.

Pristine snowflakes, whole galaxies, on dark coat-sleeves.
Be wary of things that are purely symbolic.

You have to leave yourself if you want to write a poem—
but when you have written it, the poem is all about you.

The purpose of art is transparency.
The woman at the station speaks loudly, laughing, into her phone.

Too much art, and a pigeon will break its neck.
No one recognizes the language. The woman's speech is pure music.

If you stare long enough at the cement, the cement will not stare back.
The railroad tracks go past the edge of the city.

Who knows where? The paths of coyotes in the snow
on the frozen North Saskatchewan have nothing to do with vinyl siding.

Gary Snyder described urban-sprawl houses as biped boxes.
People on the train ignore the large windows

and gaze into the little ones they hold in the palms of their hands.
Lightning chooses tall buildings, not the other way around.

Some people tremble with fear when a crow walks across their shadow.
When they dry out, sidewalks change from green to grey.

An even smaller number of people are born with black feathers.
When I was little, I was waterproof.

they worship and weep and sing.
Some archaeologists think the lines depict feathers.

Trevor Herriot: Who is that fierce little pagan within us,
who keeps driving us out into the thorny plains,

away from the clapboard enclosures of civilized life?
Every time you open your eyes,

they have a different face: the breathing cosmos.
Bears seem to have returned, after the human artists,

and added more scratches to the ones already there.
The illusion of the individual self.

The feathered crown is a crown of sunrays. A halo.
Remember the man with the head of a bird?

Just when you think you have it all figured out,
there's another surprise in the study of cave art.

When there's a wildfire, yellow grass blackens.
Then it greens. The mind is already in the next place:

does that mean it doesn't wander?
Over their morning coffee, firefighters study colour theory.

When they sleep, they dream in black and white.
Pointillism: the heartbeat loud in the throat.

Vandalizing valuable works of art is a new form of protest.
If they were alive today, the artists themselves

would probably get it. But art collectors don't!
The pressure of the breath: stare at a painting long enough,

and you're in it. You look out at the strange person
who is staring in at you.

THE LAST STANZA FEATURES
A HOPEFUL INVERSION OF THE FIRST

The moon sees her round, silver self in the dark water.
The frog pond is her looking glass.

And if she looks closely, she can see her reflection
in the shining black back of the beetle.

When you say a word over and over,
it starts to sound like noise, like nothing.

A disturbance into words, a pillow of old words,
says Samuel Beckett; how hideous is the semicolon.

Beetle beetle beetle beetle beetle beetle beetle.
But what does it sound like if you never say it?

Where can I find a man who has forgotten words,
says Chuang Tzu, so I can have a word with him?

If you treat a sonnet like a clay pigeon,
the result probably won't be a haiku. But you can try!

THE MOMENT WHEN THE METAPHOR
BECOMES THE THING ITSELF

Writing teaches writing. But last night's words
have rearranged themselves on the page.

A song composed of fragrances: the forest is breathing.
The ministering land. Cats are loath to discuss God,

says Gwendolyn MacEwen. But a cat's purr
is a healing mechanism. We exhale vowels.

I fell asleep with a book on my chest: its spine became my spine,
its pages became my lungs. Each word a little circle of air.

A memory of a tree. Punctuation marks are drawings
of the momentary sculptures we make out of our breath.

How in the world is Jacques Derrida getting so much mileage
out of that story about standing naked in front of the cat?

He announces that he has moved Buddhism
from Religion to Philosophy.

We've already had this talk, before he was hired.
They probably had it before I was hired, too.

We concluded it's easier for customers if it's in Religion.
He wasn't thinking about customers.

He never stops talking about himself
and his undergraduate philosophy classes.

He wears controversial T-shirts. He name-drops.
I think he's ridiculous, a caricature,

but I behave the same way
when someone comes in asking for a copy of *The Secret*.

I assume he hasn't seen much Buddhist art,
with all its gods and demons, heavens and hells,

but this is not a conversation
for a Friday afternoon staff meeting.

How to distinguish British Columbians from Albertans?
Look at their choice of Self-Help books.

All these books keep saying life is terrible,
the world is a terrible place. Why don't I believe them?

Field poetics. Should a poem be mowed in straight lines?
Or should the line be a wild prairie?

I don't believe there is any inherent value
in the cultivation of the self, wrote Susan Sontag.

Individuality has become a synonym for selfishness.
Every form is as sensitive as a puff of smoke.

The slightest breath will alter it completely. Prairie lake poetics:
fishing lines. Snowmobiles breaking through ice.

Words catch like knitted gloves on cracked skin.
In the mirror, my father's tired face.

Here's how to double the lifespan of your socks
when they wear out: put them on upside down.

So the heel of your sock is on the top of your foot.
This gives you new soles, and windows

if you want to see your toes. There are others.
They're everywhere! Lift your arms up out of the water,

and join your hands over your head, so your reflection
in the little chrome circle at the end of the bathtub

resembles the National Film Board of Canada logo.
You see? Your whole body is an eye.

Gaston Bachelard says houses are like the human psyche.
The top floor is airy, elevated, light.

The word "window" means "wind's eye."
The basement is dark, subterranean, subconscious.

Things we grow up being afraid of.
A house is aligned vertically, with an upstairs and a downstairs.

The main floor is horizontal. It opens up to the sidewalk,
and the street, and connects us to everyone else.

Including the trees, who have similar levels and alignments.
Some metaphors are so powerful

they've become associated with the sacred.
In the middle of the night the house makes noises.

This is a duplex, a house divided so to speak, so who knows
what the neighbours are doing. Especially at four in the morning.

Why are they up so early? They have a baby.
Or was that a house noise, a moaning of water pipes?

Sometimes a floor creaks even when no one's walking on it.
Like it's been holding on to that thought.

NAME THE STREETS AFTER
THE TREES YOU CUT DOWN

Some homes have no voices.
Some voices wander around looking for homes.

There's clock watching, and there's broken-clock watching.
Have mercy on us, we who mistake

the operation of an internal combustion engine
for a rite of passage into adulthood.

All writers learn from the dead, says Margaret Atwood.
If you need a laugh, read the comments.

If you want a happy ending, try A.
If you can use the app for free, you are the product.

If you say in a poem, "grass is red."
If you could live anywhere in the world,

and at any point in history, what would you choose?
Beware of anyone who answers here and now.

II

THE HIDDEN MYSTERY SCHOOL
IS HOLDING AN OPEN HOUSE

THE HIDDEN MYSTERY SCHOOL
IS HOLDING AN OPEN HOUSE

Be still, my heart: these great trees are prayers.
The leaf becomes flower when it loves,

says Rabindranath Tagore, and the flower becomes fruit
when it worships. Holy communion for the bears!

The prickle of ice and dried leaf on warm
and unsuspecting skin. The shiver when you expect hot

and get cold: to be kissed on the mouth by a goddess.
The halo of fall colours! The noise of the universe.

The thought of everyone lolling around
in an emotionally satisfying faith is repugnant to me,

says Flannery O'Connor.
I thought we were supposed to feel this in our bones.

King Arthur's name comes from *artos*, meaning bear.
Beowulf means "bee wolf," which means bear. And so on.

The bear constellation, which wanders hourly up and down,
moves and turns the heavens.

What dreams in just two lines!
You must see the writing as emerging, says Margaret Atwood,

like a long scroll of ink from your finger.
To harmonize the whole is the task of art:

the gift of divining the inner life in everything.
Write without distractions, says the digital screen.

You're not hearing the ocean, or your own heartbeat.
Black flowers blossom in the night:

one might distinguish two separate imaginations.
Around the musical note, the bell. Around the singing bird, the song.

Pollen-coloured warblers in sun-coloured branches.
All the birds agreed to keep the light

and carry the darkness under their wings. What about you?
What are you carrying? Magpies lean from branches,

hook and pull with their talons at your memory of it.
The desire for otherness: under the body

of a mythic spider, literature becomes personal.
Harold Rhenisch: Language isn't all for human ears,

because humans didn't invent it. They just paid attention to it.
The sound of waves. Seed syllables.

The picking of the apple from the paradise tree
may be compared with the theft of fire.

Seeds sewn into garment hems. A tent with three doors.
The word for the rustle of wind in leaves.

and the pregnant clouds. The wind parts pages
down to the spine, leaves down to the branch,

hair down to the scalp. To contemplate
comes from the word *templum*: temple.

Do you remember catching raindrops in your mouth?
Intermediaries between the human

and more-than-human worlds. The Muse.
As the poet stands open-mouthed in the temple of life,

says Denise Levertov, contemplating their experience,
there come to them the first words of the poem.

If there is to be a poem. Mud puddles:
sidewalks and avenues open their eyes. Then wider.

SOME PEOPLE'S DAYS ARE STILL
PUNCTUATED BY CHURCH BELLS

We are always in danger of drawing our own eye,
according to Wendy Doniger,

for we depict our own vision of the world
when we think we are depicting the world.

My least favourite part of travelling: returning home again.
Don't let the impatience, don't let the unhappiness,

make its way into the writing.
But what is a poem if not a string of funnels and sponges?

A tangle of strings, pulled taut?
Cat's cradle. Caught.

The most intense experiences in our lives
are the ones that didn't happen.

we have never forgiven the wolves.
We keep drawing smaller and smaller circles.

Colour has been disappearing from the world:
children act out their parents' wounds.

I follow a thread. My ankles have wings.
There are antlers on my head. Who am I?

I don't remember that, but it's in my handwriting.
What if it turns out, as Robert Bly wrote,

that we can meet the Divine only at night?
And it leads back to where I began.

Darkness is an endangered species: we hunt the night.
Call it progress. Anyway, you don't want *it*,

you want the feeling that comes *after* it. Friday is a mirror.
The dark pines of your mind reach downward,

says Gwendolyn MacEwen. You dream in the green
of your time. A forest is a mirror.

Do you like *A* because it feels like *B*,
or do you like *B* because it feels like *A*?

Wanda Coleman: there is no degree
for what is learned in the dark. A book is a mirror.

So is a bed. A chair. A glass of water. The entire room,
the entire skull. The exquisite corpse approach

to post-secondary education. The day after:
an entire Saturday morning in boxes, one after another.

With the cellar as its roots, and a nest on its roof:
the house of dreams. Universal design.

The dark red light in the upstairs window,
and the orange room beside it. The setting sun is forged,

hammered thin, on the horizon.
Do grey pigeons know they're the colour of rainclouds?

Do white pigeons know they're the colour of snow?
The sunless soft fold of skin under a baby bird's wing.

The thin, pale skin of your eyelids:
the heaviest veils between waking and sleeping.

And what is a door? The door handle,
says Juhani Pallasmaa, is the handshake of the building.

The cricket in the tree at dusk sings bright green songs
about the sun. I reach out. I open.

and the lovesick moon follows.
Tree-climbing is a transformation symbol.

Leaves are nothing more and nothing less
than flat fingers, playing xylem-phones.

Churches and churchyards are especially important for lichen.
We're studying to become proficient

on machines that don't matter. Prosthetic imaginations.
Technologies for all the wrong kinds of trances.

Selah Saterstrom: A horizon confesses another horizon.
Something larger than thought: the wind in the grass.

Digital recordings of the weather elsewhere,
loons on a lake or rain on bamboo,

help people sleep at night.
Bear: someday spiritual people, who never eat meat,

will claim you as one of their own.
Breaking a mirror is good luck, for the fish.

Bear: someday scholarly people, who never leave the city,
will claim you never existed.

That baby dolphin was so cute, everyone wanted a selfie.
How do they feel when they see

those photographs now? Hey, don't look at me!
You're the one who can't wait for the world to end.

The moon is a callus. It's been that kind of month.
It grows, it hurts, you stop noticing it.

I am a mountain ash tree with fermented berries.
You are a Bohemian Waxwing murmuration.

Which wild mushroom did I eat when I was first learning to walk?
Which version of this story is true?

The coin taken from the fish's mouth
is stamped with the imprint of a fish.

When language addresses itself, is that poetry?
A tent in the wind, sheets in the tent, a dream of sailing.

I close the book, turn off the light.
You are the words that keep breathing in the dark.

Shadows on the curtains—every night a different tree.
In her dreams her toes reach down into the soil,

and her fingers reach up to the sun. Book reviewers call that a cliché.
The poplars outside her windows have the same dreams.

Does that make the book reviewers right?
Every day, the Minotaur sat and stared at the wallpaper.

She thought she saw someone moving behind the floral pattern.
I have ceased to question stars and books, says Hermann Hesse.

I have begun to listen to the teachings my blood whispers to me.
The walls itch, and what help are the pictures in their frames?

Little birds of an idea: magpie nests are shaped like brains.
The trees keep their brains underground.

The sound of a landscaping rake on a smooth bed of topsoil.
A subconscious poem. Subterranean.

The birthplace of soil, the language of grass and sand.
Stories told by bison, and by horses. But who's listening?

Edmonton: dusty sunrise over duck ponds and dump trucks.
Farmers displaced by this construction,

and Indigenous peoples displaced by the farmers before that.
Whole populations manipulated by industrial agriculture.

And forgetting. The narrative of progress: hoodoos of the mind.
The sound of a landscaping rake on a smooth bed of topsoil—

but there's one small rock. A persistent note. A ringing,
repetitive clunk. The vibration travels up the aluminum rake handle,

through your work gloves, to your bones. Again. Again.
This is not teaching a stone to speak. It's teaching a human to cease.

THERE IS A TAME, AND ALSO
A WILD, SIDE TO THE HUMAN MIND

Adam means "dirt," and Eve means "life."
Now let's talk again about the story of the rib.

You know how a sunrise brightens, colours,
burnishes the top branches of trees?

That's how a pileated woodpecker must feel all the time.
Two different worlds:

on the screen, wolf pups play happily
with the spinal column of a freshly killed deer.

The filmmaker is admonished by the conference organizers
for not including a trigger warning.

He confesses, he doesn't know what that means.
Why would he? He lives with wolves!

Every blade of grass has its angel
that bends over it and whispers, "Grow, grow."

THE MOON WILL STILL BE
AN OBJECT OF WONDER,
EVEN AFTER IT'S PRIVATE PROPERTY

We are a constellation in the grass,
looking up at the Milky Way.

There is something like the sound of a drum.
Linked haiku: rain flows off the rooftop.

The quiet, rhythmic song a fisher sings while mending. Nets.
Everything is waiting just below the surface.

A boatload of moonlight: imagine an entire religion
pretending its god is not a gambler.

A hot bath draws a crescent moon across my stomach.
I close my eyes and soak with stars.

THE WORD "TREE" IS NOT ADEQUATE

The word "star" is not adequate. There were four of us
lying on our backs in the grass, looking up at the night sky.

Planned obsolescence does not apply to stories.
The word "summer" is not adequate. Reflecting pond:

the heron's back. The stories we need most turned up,
says Martin Shaw, right on time: about five thousand years ago.

Signposts to being real human beings. Cottonwood sap,
marshy water, blossoming trees—fill your lungs with it.

The myth-woven world: our children will inherit
the choices we make today. Painted lady, green darner,

trembling aspen leaves: wings in the breeze.
Touch the bark of holy trees. Four lines forming a character,

implying the passage of time, carved on a smooth stone
then returned to Driftwood Creek.

A DOOR LETS YOU INTO THE HOUSE, AND YOU LET THE DOOR OUT

The word "curriculum" is related to "current"—
meaning to run, to flow—

we're all made of the dust from exploded stars.
Rain breaking on rocks, rocks breaking in the rain:

the laying on of hands.
To supplement formal creative writing classes,

wrote Bonnie Friedman, we need informal ones,
where students can write about

what they are most afraid to write about.
What a way to experience the world: in our own bodies.

ORNITHEOLOGY

The soul is the body's moon.
We see a coyote on our way out of the city:

an auspicious beginning. The sky fills with clouds,
and the clouds fill with dark pink morning sun.

Only in a world where there are cranes and horses,
says Robert Graves, can poetry survive.

I need to sleep, but when I drive all day
I have the worst nightmares about driving.

The writings and drawings of the inner universe.
In a Danish grave from 4000 BC,

a young woman is buried with a baby.
Whose tiny body was placed on the wing of a swan.

Road-killed pigeon—flapping all four wings,
raven outdistances magpies and crows.

Icy wind outside—three dogs snore and sigh at the end of the bed.
The book moves with the pulse in my fingertips.

Ah, cold, dry wintertime—warm coats and dandroflage shirts.
The lunar eclipse drove me to work.

The triskele made of desire paths under the High Level Bridge
is where the city of Edmonton as we know it began.

A space between trucks, a gap in the raven's wing feathers,
sun through the clouds. We paint together in my dreams.

Skittering on ice, racing powdery snow—
the dog, same colour as a dry elm leaf, chases one.

Streetlights on new snow: everything glitters like flakes of mica.
Streets become dark tunnels, lined with precious stones.

Sometimes the whole day squeezes itself in, behind your eyes,
trying to get out, trying to turn itself back

into yesterday. Or trying too soon to become tomorrow.
Sometimes tomorrow crams itself in there too.

Both days at once: the worst headaches.
To free art from its bonds to material reality,

from the nightmare of materialism:
to lose ourselves entirely in the universe of moss.

Mouse-paths in the grass, under snowbanks.
Train imagery is overused in both literature and cinema.

So how do you write about it when the train's whistle wakes you up
in the middle of the night? The love poem.

My ribs, the mattress's ribs—I can't sleep. This is a war,
says the newscaster reporting on the winter storm.

A war with Mother Nature.
When a metaphor is taken too far it becomes a projectile.

Try to talk to someone when they're snoring:
their responses are all the same. The mind races.

Happiness is only a purchase away,
but what happens when the box store runs out of boxes?

Time moves differently depending on your bedsprings.
From a net of clouds, the moon:

so much of writing is trying to remember
your thoughts from other states of consciousness.

An inexplicable need to follow
the pathways of unseeable sparks and insects in the blankets.

On the legs of ants, on ten thousand tiny insect feet,
the shadows of days move across the snow.

Martin Shaw says the stories are here, but are we?
Or are we losing the capacity to behold them?

In the spring, when the sun with its green heat melts everything,
ten thousand ants as quiet as shadows

will make new paths. If you never watched television,
what would your dreams look like?

Sometimes sweat feels like an insect
crawling between your shoulder blades.

Sometimes biting insects are attracted by sweat.
Myth is an echolocation arising from the Earth itself.

It is the sound of the Earth and its inhabitants thinking
about themselves. Itself. The boundary between body and thought.

THESE PIECES OF SEA GLASS
WERE OCEAN-TUMBLED FOR DECADES

Poetry is a bridge between one person and another,
and between the past and the present.

But the river that flows, and has always flowed,
beneath the bridge is also poetry. So why bother?

The moon you feel in your earlobe, your belly,
your inner ear, in the ocean of you. Everyone prays

to doors. Close, we petition. Open, we wish.
Close. Some days the hinges answer.

Two students taught me how to fold origami butterflies.
Then they flew away.

IF YOUR EYES WEREN'T PRISMS, WOULD YOU NOTICE?

Failure is a great teacher, someone said.
But how do the report cards work?

Get up, put on tubes of fabric. Do things with machines.
You're supposed to pretend you're not

just a little kid who grew older.
What's the word for the temperature and texture

of mud between your toes? Is it a different word
if it's your fingers? If it's sand?

I wanted a job I'd feel proud of: my own reasons to feel proud.
I wanted to sleep for 8 hours or more.

I had forgotten that about black licorice ice cream.
I saw the best minds of my generation

not necessarily destroyed, and not necessarily by madness,
but spending a lot of time talking about real estate.

THERE ARE FACES IN THE FLOWERPOTS

In the space between bricks, the sparrow nest.
Some people live in neighbourhoods too new for ghosts,

so they haunt their own houses instead.
Geographies of nowhere. People passing on the sidewalk

see their windows flickering with pale blue light.
Aside from its enormous social cost, says James Kunstler,

the whole system of suburban sprawl
is too expensive to operate, too costly to maintain,

and a threat to the ecology of living things.
In the sparrow nest, music. The language of large and small.

Sometimes people become their own poltergeists,
banging cupboards, rattling silverware,

waking themselves up in the middle of the night.
And navy-blue thread, and strands of human hair.

EVERY SASKATOON LEAF HOLDS
A GLOWING BEAD OF RAIN

Let me wake up with green skin, a foliate head.
A leaping greenly spirit: instead of words, I'll speak leaves and vines.

For me, slow-growing as a tree, spring would be the dawn,
and fall would be the dusk, of a single day.

Let me wake up as a bird, an owl, inside a hollow tree,
blinking in the warm evening dust of feathers and bones.

Or in an osprey nest high over a lakeshore, silvered with fish scales,
bright in the morning sun. A blue true dream of sky.

Let me wake up as an earthworm: my entire body
twisting with taste buds, each new vein of soil a feast.

Vibrations: the ears of my ears awake. My whole length listening.
Rain-seep will be my calendar. Daylight the colour of beets.

So much becomes dull, gives back no light.
Don Domanski: poets are instigators of new emotional patterns.

The air around us is always busy with messages:
the least we can do is try to be here.

The revelation of the self, to the self.
Words are skeleton keys to the dual universe. Cosmos and psyche.

While I stand landlocked at the bus stop,
sunrise-coloured seagulls sing about the ocean.

Adrienne Rich: a poem is an instrument for embodied experience.
Stories aren't therapy. They're oxygen! They're fish.

Animal-body rootedness, animal comprehension,
the five cups of our senses. They're lakes.

Loons. Loops. Spoons. Oyster shells. Moons. A many-islanded sea.
The universe is a whirling dervish.

III

TO BECOME WORTHY OF THE OCEAN

Saturated with dreams like a sponge in the shallows.
The sounds of colours, the vibrations of colours:

between two extremes lie the innumerable forms.
You say you don't believe in the Underworld.

Do you believe in dogs?
Everything tends towards the shape of a star.

On the other hand, there exists no purely material form.
Octopi are sentient beings. Now what do we do?

The silence goes violet. Night in our veins.
Billie Chernicoff: God wants us to know her real names.

The whole infinite expanding universe isn't all
that interested in what's going on

in this one little corner. Is it?
Loam and seeping moss and invertebrates,

hot microbes and cool fingertips of green.
Rhythms learned from hoofbeats

and from the moth people's wings.
Mycelial pathways between the roots of trees.

The celestial nectar is water.
The skin of the drum is your skin.

WHAT'S IT GOING TO BE?
MARIE KONDO, OR *TSUNDOKU*?

Can you feel it? It's the distant glitter of sunlight
on lakewater between trees, first glimpsed from the back seat,

in one of your earliest memories of summer.
I am not contained, Walt Whitman wrote,

between my hat and boots. It's a musical note,
barely audible, hovering just above your skin. Listen.

Where are you now, bookstore customer, rough-bearded
and rough-handed, buying up all the poetry?

You said you lived out in a cabin, working as a carpenter,
and in the evenings you read aloud to the stars.

So much fog on the lake, there is no distant shore—
quick! Start paddling!

IN THE POOL WHERE YOU LEAST
EXPECT IT, THERE WILL BE A FISH

He made sure that ships steered clear of the rocks,
but the lighthouse keeper's cat

decimated the island's population of small, flightless birds.
There must always be two kinds of art.

Through the course of your life, you have been home, incubator,
and food source for all manner of microscopic beings.

Including the demodicids that are currently feeding
in the follicles of your eyelashes.

The story of Jonah is also a story about the cosmic mouth.
A memory is a new cattail in early summer, beside a clear pond;

a new cattail in early summer, beside a clear pond, is a memory.
Poetry is the journal of the sea animal living on land,

wanting to fly in the air, says Carl Sandburg.
Stop waiting for the synapses, say the pebbles on the beach.

LIMN

Limnology: the day slips through our fingers.
Hands of sand hold on to the afternoon's heat

and squeeze it, not wanting to let go.
The moon on the lake opens, blinks,

and with only the slightest rising and falling
of musical notes, laughs.

The pale brown gravel road's long legs
follow the shore. Mint grows wild in the ditches.

After rain, trumpet blossoms untwist: butterfly music.
Through sliding windows, morning glories

climb cinderblock walls. The lake last night was so close
I could hear it breathe, its fingers on the glass.

APPLICATIONS WILL BE CONSIDERED
ON A ROLLING BASIS UNTIL
THE POSITION IS FILLED

Windows in houses and whole towers of glass show the sun its face
and they do it so slowly, we don't notice they're melting.

A young woman on the bus ignores the glances and the manspreading,
lost in an EPL book. Wasp and ant populations

could double because of the extended heat wave.
People in work boots and reflective vests emerge from the dark

blinking train tunnel, like miners after a night shift underground—
exhausted from the weight of the entire city on their backs.

Nodding man in crisp white shirt: even his photo ID looks
        sleep deprived.
No other species will travel so far without returning.

Bees hold each other's legs as they sleep.
The rain can make even parking lots smell good.

BOOKS COME FROM TREES,
AND NOT JUST THE PAPER

I'm going to keep on saying God save the Queen,
and as always, I'm referring to bees.

There's an energy, a buzz, a longing, a hurt.
Like water, it's a pull from inside.

To me, these are tears. To you, they're dice.
What do you do with your past selves?

Fight them or sleep with them?
An eyelid twitch, a moth at the bedside lamp.

A snowbank full of spiders.
When beets go to seed, they smell like honey.

You know? This just might work!
But we're going to need a lot more magpies.

Magpie is the man in the suit who thinks no one's looking:
snot-rocket on the sidewalk! Magpie's eyes are black ice.

Grey season is a suitable time for isolating.
The brown study of winter: concrete-coloured snow, slush,

icy roads, icy sidewalks. The brutalist architecture
of dirty snowbanks, and how we've made everything all about cars.

Psst! and I look around the tired bus.
I want it to be someone in bright colours, beckoning,

but there are only smartphone screens
and there is only blowing snow in the dark outside.

Magpie is the old man outside before dawn,
shovelling sidewalks after a snowfall. Magpie is the snowfall.

Berry seeds, chunks of apple, fish heads—bear scat beside the trail.
I write because I am angry, says Lorna Crozier.

Because I fear the passing of foxes and owls, of all beautiful things.
There is a line where landscape painters stop working

and landscape labourers begin. The boundary is most visible
in the summer. On one side of the line, we do our best

to be refreshed by the Beauty of Nature. Thin threads of language.
Spiderwebs. On the other side we do our best

to spray it, filter it, trap it, trim it, poison it, shoot it,
and shut it out. Just ask the magpies. Ask the trees and sparrows,

dandelions and rats, slugs and fungi. Thin threads.
Ask the deer. Ask the earthworms, thistles, and mosquitoes.

Sharp points of sun—a broken bottle on the sidewalk.
Time measured not in minutes or hours but in cigarettes.

Not the individual bird. The rushing walls of train tunnels,
the loneliness of shopping carts.

The erotic urgency of pigeons. Two broken bowls,
a crooked sign. What does art want?

A dog barks in the middle of the night.
The entire street listens. How could it be any other way?

The past clings to you. Haunting. You cling back.
A large oak leaf fits perfectly on a human face.

Mural on Granville Island: "The Birds of False Creek."
Andrea Menard: You are here to sing to the waters.

THE GREAT CHAIN-LINK FENCE OF BEING

We think that's a song, but the cicada is naked
and trying to hold on.

Describe snow to someone who has never experienced it before:
in the tracks of caterpillars and dump trucks in the clay,

hoofprints of deer. The air heavy between us.
Another winter construction job—my beard is turning white.

Below minus thirty, each breath almost hurts.
Trees are house larvae. Is that too anthropocentric?

Falling snow, rising cigarette smoke—meeting before work.
And that's us, right in the middle!

The spring tree—slowly—crumples its fists at winter.
Crows and shredded black plastic on barbed wire.

A little boy in the clear green stream:
up to his elbows in tadpoles, up to his knees in summer.

Headachey dreams keep waking me up. Seen from a paper airplane:
desks, small black chalkboards. Children are writing

big, loopy letters in white chalk. What does this have to do
with the forest fires up north? The air outside is brown. Gold.

Tawny grammar. The whole city is a wet smouldering campfire.
There is a large cat, a lynx judging by the tufts of fur on its ears,

sitting at the teacher's desk. The kids don't seem to notice.
There is no guarantee that any school anywhere in the whole world,

says Gary Snyder, can give a child an education
that will be of practical use in twenty years. I'm looking down on all this.

The strange thing is, I just keep flying. I'm up in the air,
in the middle of the room, but I don't reach the other side.

Musical notes. Cat's paws of water. The nocturnal city:
it's raining, and now the air smells even more like burning.

So much is changing so fast—except, perhaps,
for caribou migrations and the berry ripening.

IN FACT, HUMAN LIFE IS RATHER LIKE AN ENORMOUS, ILL-LIT AQUARIUM

Caribou used to live here. Coal miners, too.
Only one of these things is considered history.

Not all creeks and rivers sound like the blues.
It's spiderweb-sensitive, but crow-loud:

memory is a bird-dark tree.
Barely more than synapses and stories.

Riddles! Is wind really just the spaces between
the leaves? The bottle won't open

if you turn its lid that way, or that way.
Men on recreational vehicles

eat up the trails with their rubber tires.
They leave more sand dunes than they find.

Do you see nothing watching from under the water?
Every person in the country can fit inside their cars.

A flower is bigger on the inside than it is on the outside.
Mirza Ghalib wrote that for the raindrop, joy is entering the river.

And for the river, joy is entering the ocean.
Inside every flower is an entire summer.

I'm staying in a travel trailer for an entire August. I'm trying to write,
but these flies keep bumping their heads on the ceiling.

If you make it any smaller, can you still call it a poem?
Rivers are cool, strong hands that massage the ocean's sun-warmed back.

And raindrops are the ocean's warm fingertips
that reach down and trace patterns on the river's bare legs.

We call this the hydrologic cycle. There are better words.
Flowers don't bloom, they spill. They overflow.

Dandelions open with a sound
that only some insects can see.

Can you invent a new word for me?
Slugs leave trails like silver threads, like unrolled pearls.

I am not following you,
we just have the same taste in sidewalks.

Eye contact with a hatching bird:
the world is made of stories.

If you want me again, look for me under your boot-soles.
The one about the hunter who shot a pure white moose:

what if Moses had gone home to get an axe,
then cut down the burning bush?

The scientist is only the magician of the daylight world,
says Stephen Larsen. An exile from the mythological.

Is this true? A poem is a place of thinking.
A poem is a place for thinking. Plant a pole in the ground

and for a whole year trace the path of its shadow.
Bitter milk of dandelion stems, bright powder

from their flowers. Acidity of ants. All these things
on your fingertips: fern crescendos. The sweetness

of new grass and nettle juice. Prose is walking;
poetry is dancing. Is there any empirical data to support this?

Learn about the pine from the pine.
The first cathedrals, the forests, were not entirely forgotten.

Take a picture of the sun every day for a year,
always at the same hour, and from the same location.

In a few hundred years, maybe humans and dogs
will be given an opportunity to start over.

The words *secret* and *sacred* are siblings, says Mary Ruefle.
Clowns and fools were once considered holy.

I once saw a man flip a pizza in the air.
People say dogs can smell fear. It's probably sweat.

They're probably seeing facial expressions, hand gestures.
Nonverbal communications. Palm-reading.

Besides, how many generations, do you think,
before dogs can speak human languages? Call your spirit back.

Let go of the pain you are holding, says Joy Harjo.
Ask for forgiveness. The pure white rabbit in morning snow.

I DEVELOPED AN INFALLIBLE SYSTEM
OF DIVINATION, USING HOARFROST

But I'd rather stay indoors and keep warm.
The secrets are still safe.

Men first wore ties because they were afraid of buttons,
then they discovered other things to be afraid of.

Times change. They've circled back to buttons.
The sunset in a glass of water:

what would you like most to change about yourself?
All that matters is that your source material

has plenty of text to manipulate and redact.
The method is simple: take a page, cut it down the middle,

and then again horizontally across the middle.
A sundial of pine needles on the snow.

The first rule of architecture: demons travel in straight lines.
A man walks into a forest. Who walks back out?

A child climbs up into the branches of a tree,
but first the tree must climb up into the branches of the child.

The dream of flight, the memory of water.
Light is the wind that fills the sail that turns the world.

The imagination needs animism: robes of woven grass
and feathers, moss blankets.

Keep on looking at yourselves, the shopping mall says.
If a business school was a person, it would be a sociopath.

The mall speaks in mirrors. But not well. Not fluently.
The true eye of the earth is water: unexplored pools of liquid light.

And then it begins to burn. In the ancient world,
sheepskin was used to collect gold from streams.

The Golden Fleece!
Who watches me here—it was Joyce who asked,

but everyone was thinking it—
Who ever anywhere will read these written words?

Signs on a white field.
The highway was built on an earlier road,

which was built on an even earlier, older path,
first used by sheep or deer.

Hoofprints under the concrete.
Forest fires above. We walk through ourselves.

A LIFETIME OF STANDING OUT
IN THUNDERSTORMS

Trees with their roots in the sky:
there is no such thing as inner peace.

For language to have meaning, said Thomas Merton,
there must be intervals of silence somewhere,

to divide word from word and utterance from utterance.
The talk that rain makes by itself.

The clock was invented so monks could pray on the hour.
Imagine a sculpture you work on every day:

the tortured gestures of the apple trees.
A universe waits for existence. Why mourn for a cocoon?

Waves are the practice of water:
the fog comes on sabre-toothed tiger feet.

I'M IN THE SHADOW OF A GIANT, MYTHICAL TREE

and what happens to it, happens to me.
Night through foggy windows: music of the spheres.

The dog as writing companion: a musance.
Both an inspiration and a distraction.

More than half the life on Earth is in the soil. Forgive us,
O bee in your squash-flower trousers!

Forgive us. Psyche, the goddess of the soul,
is also the word for butterfly.

The skies are full of embers. Occulted moon and stars.
A smoke ceremony: a prayer for rain.

The veins of a leaf. If the soul is a spark,
please direct me to the fire.

Caragana pods crackle. Twist. Cosmic spirals.
The slanted morning sun adds autumn colours

early to the maple tree. The sun has rested longer
in the folds and creases of certain leaves:

the tea ceremony. The spiral is the moon.
The great function of poetry, says Bachelard,

is to give us back the situations of our dreams.
The snoring afternoon: a blanket made of dogs.

WHEN YOU NEED TO WALK OUT
INTO THE NIGHT OF YOURSELF

To muse: from the word for muzzle, snout, to sniff about,
to stand with one's nose in the air.

Night sounds your tent did not insulate you from:
smooth round river rocks.

Wildness is the state of complete awareness,
says Gary Snyder. That's why we need it.

The presence of pelican and osprey and gray whale in our lives.
This land is deer-coloured. This place belongs to the deer.

Memory is what runs from you, disappears in green stillness.
Your future plans run, too. The deer is desire.

Voices of chickadees and nuthatches.
The function of the dream: the chipping of a piece of stone.

THERE WAS LIGHTNING THIS MORNING, BUT YOU MISSED IT

How to tell if someone is lying to you:
how to turn into a tree.

The Bible verses with the talking serpent are literal,
but the part about forgiving everyone's debt

is just a metaphor.
We're all rectangled. We're all animals,

either trying to remember
how to be animals, or trying to forget.

Pain moves through families
until someone is ready to feel it.

The roots snapped under plough blades
with sounds like gunshots, and sometimes screams.

The last time I saw a snake,
it was cut in half by a lawn mower.

REQUIRED READING FOR THE REVOLUTION

If poetry is not dangerous, why do tyrants kill poets?
If poetry is dangerous, why do we give it to children?

Marbles on a linoleum floor, pockets full of crabapples.
The sound of coins in a tall glass jar.

If you've ever been up to your elbows in a frog pond,
you understand at least a couple important poets.

When you're a child, one summer is a large percentage of your life.
That percentage keeps getting smaller.

If your linen closet is near a window,
sometimes you'll find yourself unfolding moonlight.

A POEM IS MADE OF NIGHTS

and a night is made of poems.
The connective tissue between two people.

Between you and the dark, and the morning.
A spider's web that stretches to the moon,

or at least up into the sky and out of sight.
Mooring, morning, mourning:

the earth's tears are light.
They fall upwards and we awaken.

The first thing we do is think of someone
and wonder where they are.

If you write about someone,
that means you love them.

Why not just tell them you love them?
A poem is made of distances.

Page 3

"The Raven-Necklaced Sky" was previously published in *Canadian Literature*, issue 257, January 2025.

The phrase "A lie breathed through silver" is attributed to C.S. Lewis in Humphrey Carpenter's *J.R.R. Tolkien: A Biography*, HarperCollins, 2016.

Page 4

"The root is the mysterious tree. It is the subterranean, inverted tree," and "For the root, the darkest earth [...] is also a mirror" are both from Gaston Bachelard's *On Poetic Imagination and Reverie: Selections from the Works of Gaston Bachelard*, translated by Collette Gaudin, Bobbs-Merrill Company, 1971.

Page 8

The Ben Okri quotation is from *Birds of Heaven*, Weidenfeld & Nicolson History, 1996.

Page 9

Title is from Jack Kerouac's "Belief & Technique For Modern Prose: List of Essentials" https://www.writing.upenn.edu/~afilreis/88v/kerouac-technique.html.

Page 11

"Walking is an indicator species [...] and unhindered bodies" quotation is from Rebecca Solnit's *Wanderlust: A History of Walking*, Penguin, 2001.

The comparison of art and islands of wilderness is from Gary Snyder's "Writers and the War Against Nature" in *Back on the Fire: Essays*, Counterpoint, 2008.

Page 13

"A poem can fly" and "A poem can be in two places at once" are from Afric McGlinchey's *Poem as Totem*. https://africmglinchey.wordpress.com/page/3/.

Page 14

The Sophie Strand quotation is from *The Flowering Wand: Rewilding the Sacred Masculine*, Inner Traditions, 2022.

Page 18

"What a strange machine [. . .] sighs, laughter, and dreams" is from *Zorba the Greek* by Nikos Kazantzakis, Faber & Faber, 2008.

Page 20

"Train lines" was previously published in *Dispatches from the Poetry Wars*, June 15, 2018. https://wayback.archive-it.org/12142/20201110001949/https://www.dispatchespoetrywars.com/poetry/7-poems-by-kelly-shepherd.

Page 21

"Who is that fierce little pagan within us" question is from Trevor Herriot's *Jacob's Wound: A Search for the Spirit of Wildness*, McClelland & Stewart, 2004.

Page 23

The Samuel Beckett quotation is from *Watt*, Grove Press, 2009.
The Chuang Tzu quotation is from *The Complete Works of Chuang Tzu*, translated by Burton Watson, Terebess Asia Online. https://terebess.hu/english/chuangtzu3.html.

Page 24

"Cats are loath to discuss God" is from Gwendolyn MacEwen's "Magic Cats" in *Magic Animals: Selected Poems Old and New*, Macmillan, 1974.

Page 26

The quotation is from Susan Sontag's *At the Same Time: Essays and Speeches*, Picador, 2007.

Page 29

The Margaret Atwood quotation is from *Negotiating with the Dead: A Writer on Writing*, Anchor, 2003.
"If you want a happy ending, try A" is from Margaret Atwood's short story "Happy Endings" in *The Nelson Introduction to Literature*, 2nd edition, Nelson, 2004.
The phrase "If you say in a poem, 'grass is red'" is from Louis Dudek's "Poetry for Intellectuals" in *The Poetry of Louis Dudek: Definitive Collection*, Dundurn Press, 2000. Reprinted with permission.

Page 33

The Rabindranath Tagore quotation is from *Stray Birds*, Macmillan, 1916.
The Flannery O'Connor quotation is from a letter in the *Collected Works of Flannery O'Connor*, Library of America, 1988.

Page 34

"You must see the writing as emerging [...] from your finger" is from Margaret Atwood's *The Blind Assassin*, Seal Books, 2001.
"To harmonize the whole is the task of art" is from Wassily Kandinsky's *Concerning the Spiritual in Art*, translated by M.T.H. Sader, Dover Publications, 1977.

Page 35

The Harold Rhenisch quotation is from "The Birth of Language on Mara Lake" in *Okanagan Okanogan*, September 10, 2013. https://okanaganokanogan.com/2013/09/10/the-birth-of-language-on-mara-lake.

Page 36

"As the poet stands [...] If there is to be a poem" is from Denise Levertov's "Some Notes on Organic Form" in *20th-Century Poetry & Poetics*, 4th edition, Oxford University Press, 1996. The original quotation uses the pronouns he/him.

Page 37

The Wendy Doniger quotation is from *The Implied Spider: Politics and Theology in Myth*, Columbia University Press, 1998.

Page 38

The phrase "we can meet the Divine only at night" is from Robert Bly's *More Than True: The Wisdom of Fairy Tales*, Henry Holt & Company, 2018.

Page 39

Permission to use the quote from Gwendolyn MacEwen's poem "Dark Pines under Water," was provided by David MacKinnon. (Originally from *The Shadow-Maker*, Macmillan, 1972.)
The Wanda Coleman quotation is from "Things No One Knows" in *Wicked Enchantment: Selected Poems*, Black Sparrow Press, 2020.

Page 40

"The door handle is the handshake of the building" is from Juhani
Pallasmaa's *The Eyes of the Skin: Architecture and the Senses*, Wiley, 2012.

Page 41

"A horizon confesses another horizon" is from Selah Saterstrom's *Ideal
Suggestions: Essays in Divinatory Poetics*, Essay Press, 2017.

Page 44

The Hermann Hesse quotation is from "Hermann Hesse's Arrested
Development" by Adam Kirsch in *The New Yorker*, November 12, 2018.
https://www.newyorker.com/magazine/2018/11/19/hermann-hesses-
arrested-development.

Page 46

Title is from Gary Snyder's "Writers and the War Against Nature" in *Back
on the Fire: Essays*, Counterpoint, 2008.

Page 48

"The stories we need [...] five thousand years ago" is from Martin Shaw's
Scatterlings: Getting Claimed in the Age of Amnesia, White Cloud Press,
2016.

Page 49

The Bonnie Friedman quotation is from *Writing Past Dark: Envy, Fear,
Distraction and Other Dilemmas in the Writer's Life*, Harper Perennial,
1994.

Page 50

The Robert Graves quotation is from *The White Goddess: A Historical
Grammar of Poetic Myth*, Faber & Faber, 1961.

Page 54

The Martin Shaw quotation is from "Accessing the mundus imaginalis with
the modern mind" by Tammy Gan in *Advaya*. https://advaya.life/
articles/accessing-the-mundus-imaginalis-with-the-modern-mind.

Page 56

"I saw the best minds of my generation" is from Allen Ginsberg's *Howl and Other Poems*, City Lights, 1956.

Page 57

"Aside from its enormous social cost [...] the ecology of living things" is from James Howard Kunstler's *Geography of Nowhere: The Rise and Decline of America's Man-Made Landscape*, Simon & Schuster, 1993.

Page 58

The three phrases "A leaping greenly spirit," "A blue true dream of sky," and "the ears of my ears awake" are from "i thank You God for most this amazing" by e.e. cummings, in *Xaipe*, Oxford University Press, 1950. Reprinted with permission.

Page 59

The Don Domanski quotation is from "Poetry and the Sacred" in *Selected Poems 1975–2021*, Xylem Books, 2022.

The Adrienne Rich quotation is from *What Is Found There: Notebooks on Poetry and Politics*, W.W. Norton & Company, 2003.

Page 63

"God wants us to know her real names" is from Billie Chernicoff's "Luminous Failures" in *Minor Secrets*, Black Square Editions, 2022.

Page 65

The Walt Whitman quotation is from "Song of Myself" (section 7) in *Leaves of Grass*, 1892. https://www.poetryfoundation.org/poems/45477/song-of-myself-1892-version.

Page 66

"Through the course of your life [...] of your eyelashes" is from Trevor Herriot's *Jacob's Wound: A Search for the Spirit of Wildness*, McClelland & Stewart, 2004.

The Carl Sandburg quotation is from "Nine Tentative (First Model) Definitions of Poetry" in *Harvest Poems: 1910–1960*, Ecco Press, 1960.

Page 71

Title is from Henry David Thoreau's "Walking" in *The Atlantic*, 1862. https://www.theatlantic.com/magazine/archive/1862/06/walking/304674/.

The Lorna Crozier quotation is from "Who's Listening?" in *20th-Century Poetry & Poetics*, 4th edition, Oxford University Press, 1996.

Page 72

"You are here to sing to the waters" is from Andrea Menard's *Rubaboo*, Granville Island Stage, Arts Club Theatre Company, 2023. (This line from a live theatre monologue is gratefully reprinted with written permission from Andrea Menard.)

Page 74

"There is no guarantee [...] in twenty years" and "So much is changing [...] the berry ripening" are both from Gary Snyder's "Tawny Grammar" in *The Practice of the Wild: Essays*, 30th anniversary edition, Counterpoint, 2020.

Page 75

Title is from Mary Midgley's *Science and Poetry*, Routledge, 2001.

Page 76

The Mirza Ghalib quotation is from "Mirza Ghalib Best Shayari & Ghazal" in *Best Shayarii*. https://bestshayarii.com/mirza-ghalib-best-shayari-ghazal.

Page 77

"If you want me again, look for me under your boot-soles" is from Walt Whitman's "Song of Myself" (section 52) in *Leaves of Grass*, 1892. https://www.poetryfoundation.org/poems/45477/song-of-myself-1892-version.

Page 78

The Stephen Larsen quotation is from *The Shaman's Doorway: Opening Imagination to Power and Myth*, Inner Traditions, 1998.

Page 79

> The quotation is from Mary Ruefle's *Madness, Rack, and Honey: Collected Lectures*, Wave Books, 2012.

> "Call your spirit back. Let go of the pain you are holding," and "Ask for forgiveness" are from Joy Harjo's "For Calling the Spirit Back from Wandering the Earth in Its Human Feet" in *Conflict Resolution for Holy Beings: Poems*, W.W. Norton & Company, 2015.

Page 82

> The phrases "Who watches me here" and "Who ever anywhere will read these written words? Signs on a white field" are from James Joyce's *Ulysses*, Wordsworth Editions, 2010.

Page 83

> The Thomas Merton quotation is from *The Power and Meaning of Love*, Sheldon Press, 1976.

Page 85

> "The great function of poetry is to give us back the situations of our dreams" is from Gaston Bachelard's *The Poetics of Space*, Beacon Press, 1994.

Page 86

> Title is from Catherine Owen's "a Grrrr against worrying about AI" in *Ms. Lyric's Poetry Outlaws* podcast, Season 7, episode 2, December 2022.

> The quotation is from Gary Snyder's "Four Changes" in *Turtle Island*, New Directions, 1974.

ACKNOWLEDGEMENTS

There are a number of people I would like to thank:

Harold Rhenisch, for first setting me on this path with
    (among other things) the book *Two Minds*.
Sharon Thesen, for the early and encouraging reading of
    these poems.
Catherine Owen, for the manuscript assistance, and for lending me that
    line from *Ms. Lyric's Poetry Outlaws*.
Randy Lundy, for the editorial suggestions and intuition.
Shannon Parr, and everyone at the University of Regina Press, for the
    guidance and support, and for all their hard work on my behalf.
And finally, from start to finish, for the inspiration and for your patience,
    thank you to Karen.

Kelly Shepherd's second poetry collection, *Insomnia Bird* (Thistledown Press, 2018) won the 2019 Robert Kroetsch City of Edmonton Book Prize. Originally from Smithers, British Columbia, he lives and teaches on Treaty 6 territory, in Edmonton.

ᐅᓇᐸ

OSKANA POETRY & POETICS

BOOK SERIES

Publishing new and established authors, Oskana Poetry & Poetics offers both contemporary poetry at its best and probing discussions of poetry's cultural role.

Randy Lundy—*Series Editor*

Advisory Board

PREVIOUS BOOKS IN THE SERIES:

The Salmon Shanties: A Cascadian Song Cycle, by Harold Rhenisch (2024)

Wrack Line, by M.W. Jaeggle (2023)

Dislocations, by Karen Enns (2023)

The History Forest, by Michael Trussler (2022)

Synaptic, by Alison Calder (2022)

Shifting Baseline Syndrome, by Aaron Kreuter (2022)

Pitchblende, by Elise Marcella Godfrey (2021)

Red Obsidian, by Stephan Torre (2021)

Burden, by Douglas Burnet Smith (2020)

Field Notes for the Self, by Randy Lundy (2020)

Live Ones, by Sadie McCarney (2019)

Forty-One Pages: On Poetry, Language and Wilderness, by John Steffler (2019)

Blackbird Song, by Randy Lundy (2018)

The House of Charlemagne, by Tim Lilburn (2018)

Cloud Physics, by Karen Enns (2017)

The Long Walk, by Jan Zwicky (2016)

Measures of Astonishment: Poets on Poetry, presented by the League of Canadian Poets (2016)